HYMN CREATIONS

10 PIANO SOLO ARRANGEMENTS by Randall Hartsell

In honor of the 25th Anniversary
of Cross and Crown Lutheran Church
in Matthews, North Carolina

ISBN 978-1-4584-1763-3

WILLIS MUSIC

EXCLUSIVELY DISTRIBUTED BY

HAL•LEONARD®
CORPORATION
7777 W. BLUEMOUND RD. P.O. BOX 13819 MILWAUKEE, WI 53213

Visit Hal Leonard Online at
www.halleonard.com

FOREWORD

The music in this collection comes from my recent experience as a music director for a mid-sized congregation. I usually choose a prelude that is based on the tune of the first hymn; but, if I am unable to find a suitable prelude, I will arrange one myself. Many of these preludes are a part of this new book.

I often have opportunities to improvise on hymn tunes during worship services. I am free to use *rubato*, tempo changes, dramatic shifts in dynamics, and the subtle nuances of an expressive phrase to create an intimate, spiritual experience for everyone. These hymns express the freedom and intimacy of the improvisatory style.

Being creative with music composition always brings me joy and peace. Feel free to add your own creative performance ideas to this collection and translate the rich heritage and beauty of these hymn tunes to the ears and hearts of your listeners.

Randall Hartsell

CONTENTS

Amazing Grace

Words by John Newton
Traditional American Melody
Arranged by Randall Hartsell

Moderately, with motion

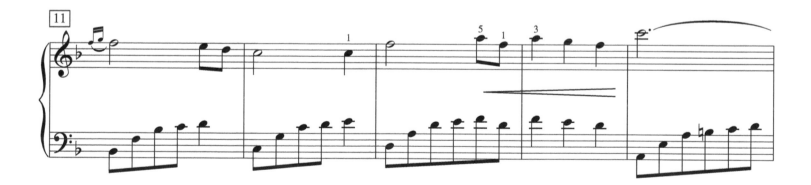

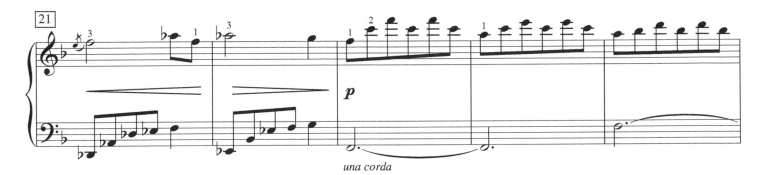

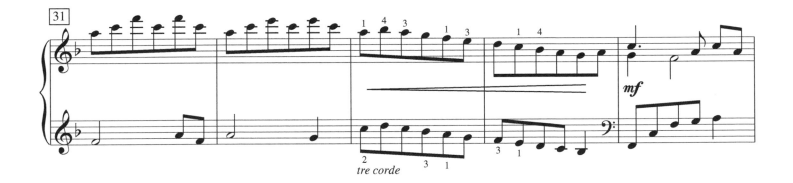

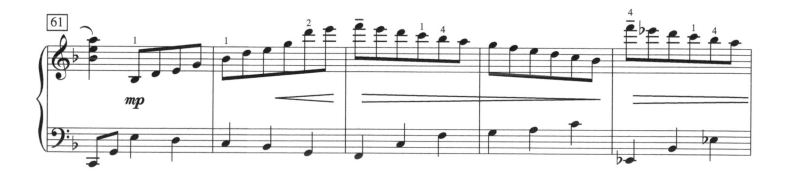

The Ash Grove
(Let All Things Now Living)

Old Welsh Air
Arranged by Randall Hartsell

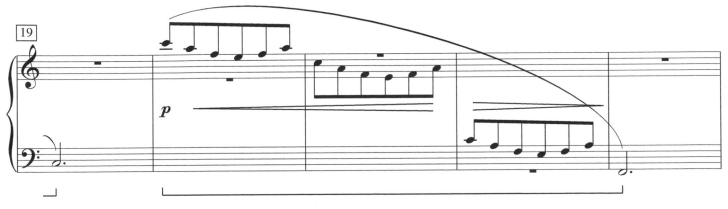

8

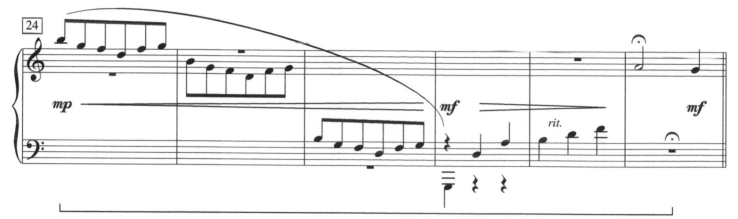

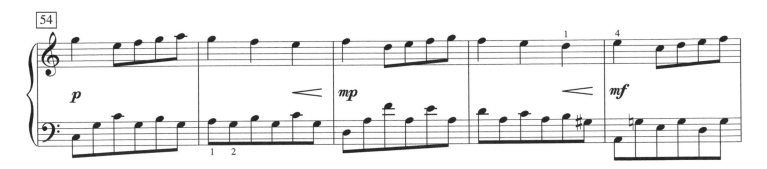

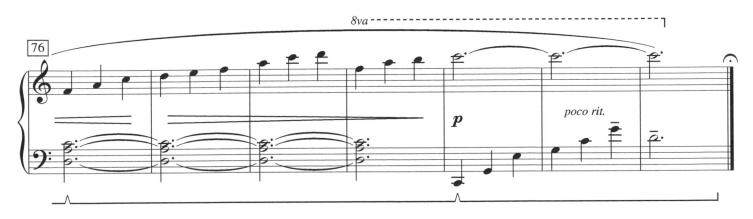

Be Thou My Vision

Traditional Irish
Translated by Mary E. Byrne
Arranged by Randall Hartsell

Moderately, expressively

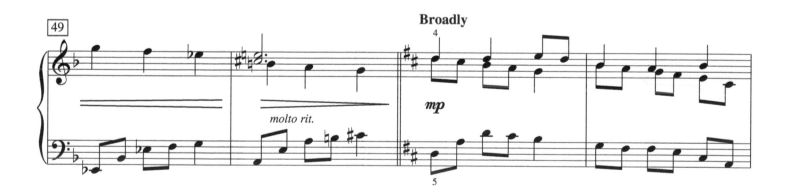

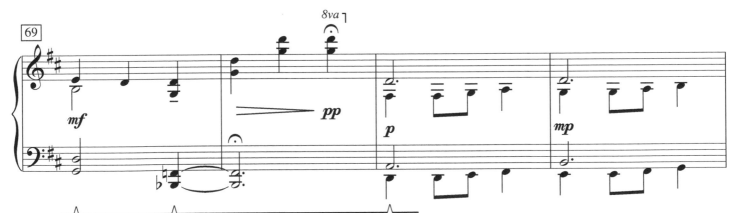

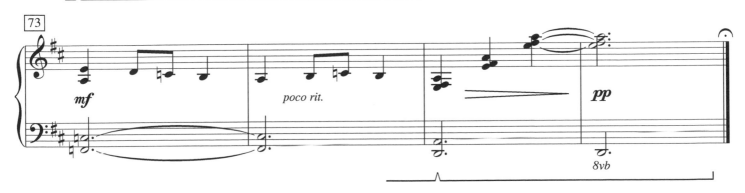

Beach Spring
(Lord, Whose Love in Humble Service)

Melody from *The Sacred Harp*, 1844
Arranged by Randall Hartsell

Andante, like a dulcimer

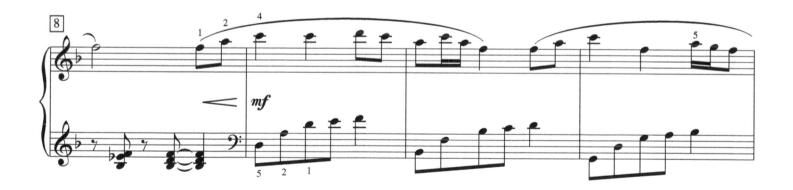

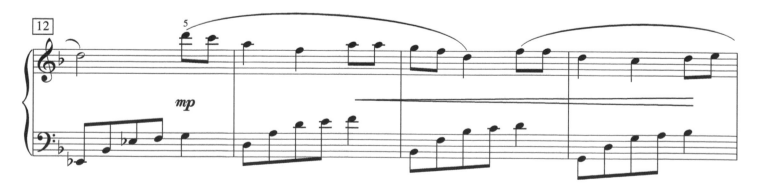

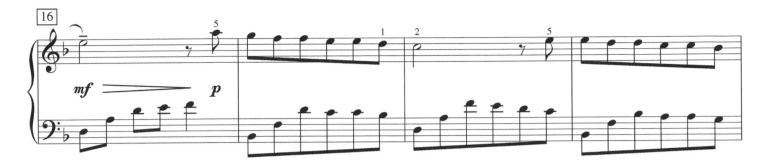

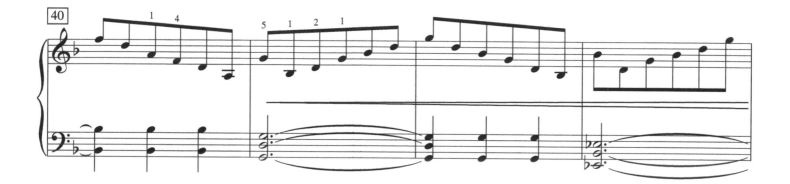

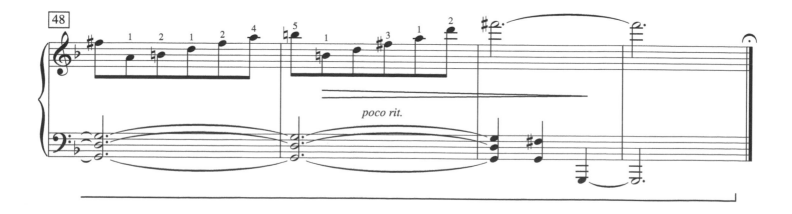

Come, Thou Fount of Every Blessing

Words by Robert Robinson
Music from John Wyeth's *Repository of Sacred Music*
Arranged by Randall Hartsell

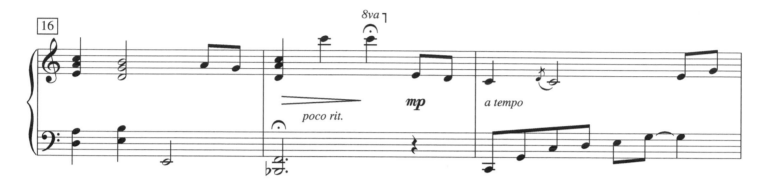

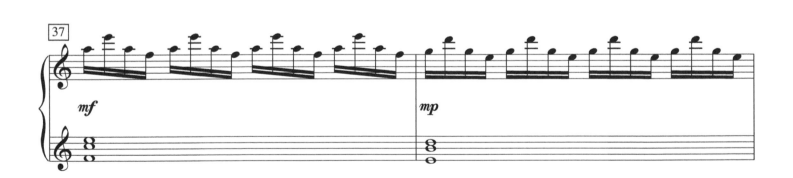

Fairest Lord Jesus

Words from *Munster Gesangbuch*
Music from *Schlesische Volkslieder*
Arranged by Randall Hartsell

Broadly

Holy, Holy, Holy

Text by Reginald Heber
Music by John B. Dykes
Arranged by Randall Hartsell

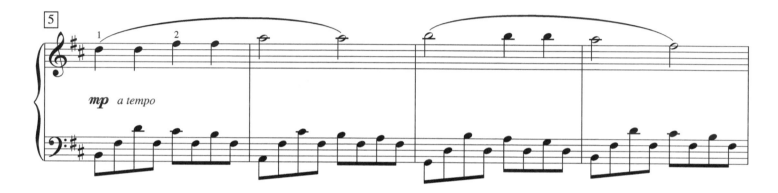

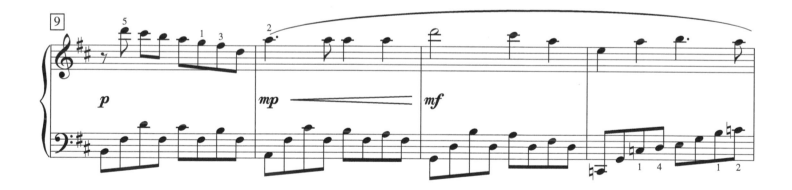

Kingsfold
(My Soul Proclaims Your Greatness)

Traditional English Melody
Arranged by Randall Hartsell

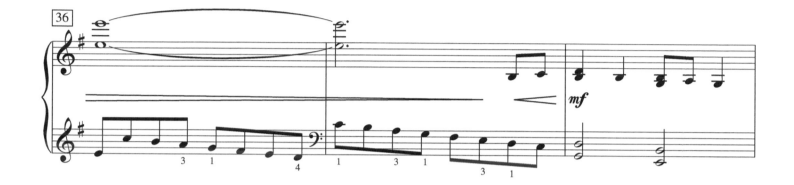

Now Thank We All Our God

German Words by Martin Rinkart
English Translation by Catherine Winkworth
Music by Johann Crüger
Arranged by Randall Hartsell

With lightness and energy

Broadly

When Morning Gilds the Skies

Words from *Katholisches Gesangbuch*
Translated by Edward Caswall
Music by Joseph Barnby
Arranged by Randall Hartsell

Moderately, expressively

BIOGRAPHY

RANDALL HARTSELL is a graduate of East Carolina University where he studied piano pedagogy and performance. His publications are influenced by many years of teaching experience, and the sweeping lyrical lines and sound technical structures in his music appeal often to both student and teacher.

Mr. Hartsell has taught piano at Pfeiffer University in Misenheimer, North Carolina, and has accompanied numerous dance classes and performances at UNC Charlotte. Currently, he operates a private studio in the Charlotte area, is a clinician for Willis Music, and serves as an officer for the Charlotte Piano Teachers Forum.